EARTH FIGURED OUT

Habitats and Biomes

Nancy Dickmann

Cavendish Square

New York

Published in 2016 by Cavendish Square Publishing, LLC
243 5th Avenue, Suite 136, New York, NY 10016

CPSIA Compliance Information: Batch #CW16CSQ

All websites were available and accurate when this book was sent to press.

Cataloging-in-Publication Data

Dickmann, Nancy.
Habitats and biomes / by Nancy Dickmann.
p. cm. — (Earth figured out)
Includes index.
ISBN 978-1-5026-0880-2 (hardcover) ISBN 978-1-5026-0878-9 (paperback)
ISBN 978-1-5026-0881-9 (ebook)
1. Biotic communities — Juvenile literature. 2. Habitat (Ecology) — Juvenile literature.
I. Dickmann, Nancy. II. Title.
QH541.14 D53 2016
577.8'2—d23

Produced for Cavendish Square by Calcium
Editors: Sarah Eason and Harriet McGregor
Designer: Paul Myerscough

Printed in the United States of America

Contents

What Is a Biome?

Every living thing lives in a **biome**. A biome is a geographic area that has different weather, landforms, and plant life than other regions. For example, **deserts** are usually considered to be a biome, and so are forests and oceans.

Within each biome you can find many different **ecosystems**. An ecosystem is not just a place; it is a system made up of the plants, animals, and nonliving things in a particular area. They depend on each other to survive. An ecosystem can be as small as a pond, or a rotting log that is home to fungi, insects, and other small animals.

For an animal or plant to survive, it must have a **habitat** that provides everything it needs. Its habitat must have food and water, and there must be shelter to protect the **organism** from **predators** and weather.

EARTH FIGURED OUT

Over many generations, animal and plant species slowly change to become better suited to their habitat. If one organism has a **trait** that helps it survive, it will pass this trait on to its offspring. Because of the helpful trait, they will be more likely to survive to pass the trait on to their own offspring. This is called **adaptation**.

Tropical grasslands, such as this one in Africa, are one of the world's major biomes.

This rock pool is an example of a small ecosystem. It is home to shellfish, seaweed, and fish, as well as many other living things.

5

Deciduous Forests

Deciduous forests are large areas of trees that lose their leaves in winter. These forests are also home to many other types of smaller plants, as well as a lot of different animals. The forests cover large areas of Europe and North America, as well as parts of Asia and Australia.

Deer, wolves, bears, and other large animals make their homes in deciduous forests. Many smaller animals, such as chipmunks, raccoons, mice, and birds, are also found there. The leaf litter on the forest floor makes a perfect home for many different insects and other **invertebrates**.

In the winter, the habitat changes as the trees' leaves die and fall to the ground. This helps the forest because the rotting leaves keep the soil rich. But in the winter, there is less food to eat. Many of the animals that live in the forests survive the winter by **hibernating**.

Hedgehogs hibernate in winter, between November and March, in nests made of piles of leaves.

A different type of forest is found to the north of the world's deciduous forests. These forests are made up of trees called conifers, which have needle-like leaves that do not fall off in winter. Winters are long and harsh, but the trees are adapted to this **climate**.

Rotting logs like this one provide a perfect home for some types of insects, as well as mosses, ferns, and fungi.

Rain Forests

Tropical rain forests are one of the Earth's most amazing biomes since they are home to a lot of different plants and animals. Found in hot, humid places, these forests have the same conditions all year round.

In a tropical rain forest, the tops of the trees form a thick layer called the canopy. It is so thick that very little light gets through to the forest floor. The plants that live below the canopy have adapted to survive with little light.

Many rain forest animals live in the trees, including birds, monkeys, sloths, snakes, bats, and insects. They fly, glide, or swing from branch to branch. Larger animals such as jaguars, gorillas, anteaters, and leopards live on the forest floor. So do smaller animals such as rodents and insects. The dappled light there helps them hide from predators or sneak up on prey.

EARTH FIGURED OUT

Rain forests are also found in cooler places, such as the northern part of the West Coast of the United States. These **temperate** rain forests get a lot of rain, and they are often home to big coniferous trees. Mosses and **lichens** also do well in this damp environment.

Tropical rain forests cover only 6 percent of Earth's surface, but they contain more than half of the world's plant and animal species.

These spider monkeys' feet and hands are adapted for grasping trees. They can also use their tails as an extra limb.

FOREST BIOMES—FIGURED OUT!

31

Forests cover 31 percent of Earth's land surface, taking up nearly 15.6 million square miles (40.4 million square kilometers). However, this area is constantly getting smaller, and each year about 20,000 square miles (51,800 sq km) are lost.

The world's biggest rain forest is the Amazon in South America. It covers an area of

2.3 million

square miles (5.9 million sq km). However, the boreal forest in Russia, made up of conifer trees, is even bigger. It covers 4.6 million square miles (11.9 million sq km) and contains more than 55 percent of the world's conifers.

The tallest living thing in the world is a tree: a coast redwood in California that measures over

375

feet (114 meters) tall.

California is also home to one of the world's oldest living things. A bristlecone pine tree called Methuselah is more than

4,800

years old.

Scientists believe that the Amazon rain forest is home to several million species of animals and plants. It has more types of animals and plants than any other place on Earth.

LET'S FIGURE OUT ...

Deserts

Rain forests make a perfect habitat for some plants and animals, but living things can also survive in much drier biomes. Deserts are areas that have very little rain—sometimes it can be many years between one storm and the next! We often think of deserts as hot and sandy, but many deserts are rocky, and some are cold. In fact, the world's largest desert is in Antarctica. It is covered in water, mostly in the form of ice, but very little new snow falls there.

Surviving in a desert is hard, but some plants and animals have adapted to make use of the small amounts of water that are found there. For example, a cactus has a lot of roots for soaking up water. Its thick, fleshy stem can swell to store large amounts of water until it is needed. Cacti have another advantage—they don't have leaves, so they can't lose water through them like other plants do.

Camels are perfectly adapted to live in the desert. They can cope with high temperatures and can go for a long time without drinking.

A mesquite tree's roots can grow more than 100 feet (30 m) underground, in order to reach water deep below the surface.

EARTH FIGURED OUT

Many desert animals, such as fennec foxes and kangaroo rats, dig burrows to escape the sun's heat. They are often nocturnal, sleeping through the hot days and looking for food at night, when it is cooler. Some desert animals can get all the water they need from their food, without needing to drink at all.

13

LET'S FIGURE OUT ...

Tundra

Another example of an extreme habitat is cold, windy tundra. Tundra is treeless places that are found in the far north of the planet. There are also some tundra zones on the tops of mountains. The tundra has long winters and very short summers, and very little rain.

Tundra soil is poor, and below the surface it is permanently frozen. Roots cannot push through the **permafrost**, so mostly smaller plants grow in tundra soil. Being short helps the plants cope with strong winds. Small shrubs, grasses, and mosses are common tundra plants. Wildflowers often bloom during the short summers.

Animals that live in the tundra are adapted to the cold climate. Many have thick layers of fur and fat to keep them warm. Some tundra animals, such as Arctic ground squirrels, hibernate during the winter. Others, such as snow buntings and other birds, **migrate** south to warmer areas.

EARTH FIGURED OUT

Some tundra animals can look very different, depending on the season. The Arctic fox, snowshoe hare, and stoat are all brown in the summer, but their fur turns white in the winter. This makes them harder to spot against the snow, which can help them hide from predators or sneak up on prey.

The musk ox's long, thick fur keeps it warm throughout the winter. Musk oxen also sometimes huddle together to keep warm.

This Arctic hare's white fur will help it hide from predators during the snowy winter.

EXTREME HABITATS—FIGURED OUT!

The average winter temperature in the tundra is

-30° Fahrenheit

(−34° Celsius). It only rises above freezing during the short summers, when it averages 37 to 54 degrees Fahrenheit (3 to 12° C).

In some hot deserts, such as the Sahara in Africa, temperatures can reach as high as

130° Fahrenheit

(54° C) during the day, though it is much colder at night. The temperature in the colder Gobi Desert in China can go up or down by as much as 60 degrees Fahrenheit (16° C) in just twenty-four hours!

Deserts get no more than

10 inches (25 centimeters) of

precipitation per year. Although its surface is dotted with bogs and ponds, the Arctic tundra gets only 6 to 10 inches (15 to 25 cm) of precipitation per year (which includes melting snow).

The saguaro cactus swells up after a rainfall, and about

90

percent of its body can be used to store water. A single cactus can hold 1 ton (0.9 metric tons) of water.

Humans can live for between three and five days without water. Some camels have been known to survive for six or seven months without water, but in the hottest summer months they can last only about five days without a drink. A camel can drink

30 gallons (114 liters) of water in just thirteen minutes!

Oceans

Oceans are the single biggest biome on Earth, covering about 71 percent of the planet's surface. The deeper you go, the darker and colder the ocean gets. The **pressure** of the water above becomes enormous, too. Without special equipment, humans can only survive in the top layers of the oceans. However, many sea creatures are adapted to go much deeper.

Scientists divide the oceans into layers, and the sunlight zone is at the top. Here, there is enough sunlight for plants, such as kelp and algae, to make food and survive. Many fish, shellfish, starfish, and other invertebrates live here, as well as mammals such as whales and dolphins.

Below the sunlight zone is the twilight zone, where there is very little light. Even deeper is the midnight zone, where there is no light at all. Many of the animals that live here are soft-bodied so they can absorb the immense water pressure without being crushed.

Coral reefs are found in the sunlight zone. They provide a habitat for a lot of different fish and other sea creatures.

EARTH FIGURED OUT

When the tide goes out, it can leave pools of seawater among the rocks and sand. These tidal pools are home to creatures such as shellfish, sea anemones, and seaweed. When the tide comes in and goes out, it brings new organisms and allows others to escape back into the ocean.

Most sea animals can get oxygen from the water, but mammals such as whales and dolphins must come to the surface to breathe.

Freshwater Biomes

Earth's rivers, ponds, and lakes hold only a small amount of water compared to the huge oceans. However, they are still important habitats. The animals and plants that live in these freshwater habitats don't need the adaptations that allow sea creatures to live in salty water.

Rivers, lakes, and ponds are home to plants such as algae. Animals that live there range from insects and fish to larger animals such as crocodiles. As well as the animals that live in the water, these freshwater habitats provide drinking water for land animals.

The water in lakes and ponds is still, but plants and animals that live in rivers must adapt to the flowing water there. Some attach themselves to the riverbed with roots or suckers. Fish called darters have a long, thin, streamlined shape that makes it easier to swim against the current, or the flow of water. Other fish have fins that help them hold on to rocks.

EARTH FIGURED OUT

A few animals are able to live in either fresh or salty water. For example, salmon lay their eggs in freshwater. The baby salmon stay there for up to four years before traveling to the oceans to find food. After several years at sea, they return to the river where they were born to reproduce.

Plants such as papyrus use their roots to hold themselves in place in the water.

Catfish often live in murky water, so they use their whisker-like barbels and sense of smell to find food.

Wetlands

Some habitats are a mix of water and land. These wetlands exist all over the world, wherever the land is **saturated** with water. This means that the soil has so much water in it that it cannot soak up any more. Some wetlands are completely covered by water for part of the year. Swamps, marshes, and bogs are all types of wetlands.

Some trees that live in wetlands have adaptations that allow them to live partly underwater. For example, a mangrove tree's tall, stilt-like roots help hold its trunk and branches out of the water. The roots also provide shelter for crabs and other animals, and the mangrove's branches hold birds' nests.

Many different reptiles and amphibians are found in wetlands, including frogs, toads, turtles, snakes, and alligators. These animals have adapted to cope with the wetlands' changing water levels.

Wetlands are home to wading birds such as herons. They walk through the water on their long legs, looking for food.

The sundew is an unusual plant found in bogs. Each of its reddish leaves is covered with hairlike spines, topped with glistening droplets that look like dew.

The droplets are sticky, and when insects come to drink them, they are trapped. The leaf's spines curl around the insects, and the leaf slowly digests them.

A swamp's trees set it apart from other wetlands. Swamps can be either freshwater or saltwater, depending on where they are.

LIVING IN WATER—FIGURED OUT!

More than **96** percent of Earth's water is found in the oceans. Only 2.5 percent is freshwater, and of this tiny amount, only 1.2 percent is liquid water that is found on Earth's surface. The rest of it is found underground, or frozen solid in **glaciers** and icecaps.

In 2014, scientists discovered a snailfish living in the oceans at a depth of **26,722** feet (8,145 m). It is the deepest fish ever found.

Only **5** percent of the salmon that make it back to the oceans after spawning survive to return and spawn a second time.

In the sunlight zone, the water temperature can range from 28 to 97 degrees Fahrenheit (−2 to 36° C), depending on the location. In the midnight zone it stays constant at

39° Fahrenheit (4° C).

Wetlands are often drained to create land for farming or houses. In the 1600s, the area that is now the United States had about 343,750 square miles (890,308 sq km) of wetlands. About

50 percent of that area remains today.

The largest protected wetland in the world is Llanos de Moxos in Bolivia. It covers more than

26,562 square miles (68,795 sq km)—about the same size as North Dakota.

Grasslands

Large areas of Earth's land are quite flat and covered in grasses, with few trees. These places are called grasslands. Grasslands in temperate places, such as in North America or Europe, have warm summers and cold winters. They are usually called **prairies** or steppes. In tropical climates, where it is warm all year round, they are called savannas.

Many prairie grasses have deep roots. This allows them to soak up as much water as they possibly can. This is important in dry climates, such as on the steppes. The grasses also have big root systems, so that grazing animals do not pull up the roots. The grasses can regrow from the roots.

Grassland animals have adaptations too. For example, there are few trees to provide cover, so many grassland animals are fast runners. Some African gazelles can reach speeds of 40 miles (64 km) per hour, but the cheetah can reach 65 miles (105 km) per hour when chasing them.

EARTH FIGURED OUT

Bison are the largest land mammals in North America. They live on the prairies, where they graze on the grasses. Their thick, shaggy coats keep them warm during the cold winters. They dig up the snow with their pointed horns during the winter to reach the plants beneath.

Large parts of North America were once covered by prairies, but a lot of this land has now been turned into farmland.

Today, bison help keep the prairies healthy, but once so many were hunted that they nearly died out. They are now making a comeback.

Habitats Under Threat

Every living thing depends on its habitat for food, water, and shelter. Unfortunately, many of the most important habitats are being lost. Humans dig up prairies to plant crops, cut down forests for their lumber, and drain wetlands to build houses. When these habitats are destroyed, the plants and animals that live there are put in danger.

Even if they are not destroyed completely, habitats can also be damaged. For example, **pollution** from factories can get into rivers, making it hard for plants and animals to survive. The **greenhouse effect** is causing water temperatures to rise, and this harms coral reefs.

Throughout Earth's history, plants and animals have adapted to survive in a lot of different habitats. But adaptations take place over a long period of time. Most plants and animals just cannot adapt quickly enough to the big changes that humans are making to their habitats. We need to work together to help protect habitats and the organisms that live there.

The tiger population has dropped by around 95 percent in the last one hundred years. Now there are only about 3,200 tigers left in the wild.

Tigers are one of the world's most endangered animals. Many of them live in jungles or forests where there are plants that the tigers can hide among as they hunt. However, these habitats are being destroyed. The humans who live nearby also hunt the same prey as tigers, leaving less food for the tigers.

We cut down anywhere between three billion and six billion trees a year, either to use the wood or to clear the land for other uses.

29

Glossary

adaptation A change in an organism, over time, that helps it survive and reproduce in a particular habitat.

biome One of the major types of landscape, such as a desert or forest.

climate The usual weather conditions in a particular place.

deciduous A tree with leaves that die and fall off each year.

deserts Very dry, sandy, or rocky areas with very few plants.

ecosystems Communities of living things, together with their environments.

glaciers Large masses of ice that move very slowly down slopes or across land.

greenhouse effect The warming of Earth's surface that takes place when heat from the sun is trapped by gases in the atmosphere.

habitat The natural environment of an animal or plant.

hibernating Sleeping through the winter in a den or burrow to save energy.

invertebrates Animals without backbones inside their bodies, such as an insects, crabs, or squid.

lichens Organisms that are made up of fungus and a form of algae living together.

migrate To travel from one region to another to find food.

organism A living thing.

permafrost Soil below the surface that is permanently frozen.

pollution The process of making land, water, or air dirty and not safe to use.

prairies Large, flat areas of land covered mainly in grasses.

precipitation Water that falls from the sky as rain, snow, sleet, or hail.

predators Animals that hunt other animals for food.

pressure A steady pushing force upon a surface.

rain forests Dense woodlands with very high annual rainfall, often with trees forming a canopy.

saturated Not able to hold any more water.

temperate Having temperatures that are not too hot or cold.

trait A characteristic that makes a living thing different from others of the same type, for example, height or eye color.

tropical Having temperatures high enough for plants to grow all year round.

Further Reading

Books

Hollar, Sherman. *Investigating Earth's Desert, Grassland, and Rainforest Biomes.* Introduction to Earth Science. New York: Rosen Education Service, 2011.

Johansson, Philip. *The Temperate Forest: Discover This Wooded Biome.* Discover the World's Biomes. Berkeley Heights, NJ: Enslow Elementary, 2015.

Johnson, Robin. *Oceans Inside Out.* Ecosystems Inside Out. New York: Crabtree Publishing Company, 2014.

Van Rose, Susanna. *Earth.* DK Eyewitness Books. New York: DK Children, 2013.

Websites

National Geographic has a really useful online encyclopedia where you can search for information on different habitats and landforms: **education.nationalgeographic.com/education/encyclopedia/?ar_a=1**

Learn more about animal adaptations and play a game to test your knowledge here: **www.planet-science.com/categories/under-11s/games/2010/09/mission-adaptation.aspx**

Find out more about the world's rain forests and how to protect them: **www.rainforest-alliance.org/kids**

Find more detail about the world's biomes here: **www.ucmp.berkeley.edu/glossary/gloss5/biome**

Index